Can God Use Me?

How to Overcome Doubt, Insecurity, and Fear

NANA BOADUM

WESTBOW
PRESS®
A DIVISION OF THOMAS NELSON
& ZONDERVAN

WestBow Press books may be ordered through booksellers or by contacting:

WestBow Press
A Division of Thomas Nelson & Zondervan
1663 Liberty Drive
Bloomington, IN 47403
www.westbowpress.com
1 (866) 928-1240

ISBN: 978-1-9736-4665-5 (sc)
ISBN: 978-1-9736-4664-8 (hc)
ISBN: 978-1-9736-4666-2 (e)

Library of Congress Control Number: 2018913920

Print information available on the last page.

WestBow Press rev. date: 12/03/2019

Contents

Dedication

To my parents, Rt. Rev. Dr. and Rev. Mrs. Comfort Anyani-Boadum. Your love, care, hard work, and legacy of faith in Jesus is a remarkable example. God bless you, Daa and Maa.

Acknowledgments

I thank God for my beloved wife, Ethel Sefakor, and our children, Nyamede (God's own) and Nana Ayeyi (Praise). Doing life with you is a privilege and a pleasure.

To my siblings, Rev. Addo, Rev. Dr. Oheneba, Kristodea, and Nicky, together with your lovely families. My nieces and nephews, Mikaela, Isabel, Daniela, Nyameye, Nesayah, Caimie, Aeliena, Elnathan, Radiance, N'adom, Judah Otumfuo: you are loved.

To the children and teens ministry of Jesus Generation – Accra, Ghana. I recall the good times we have spent together at camp meetings, all-night services, sporting activities, drasingpo's (Drama-singing-poetry events), and many more. Your teachable spirit has both encouraged and challenged me.

The world-changers at Bethlehem Green School, together with their parents and our staff. We are family!

I am thankful to Rev. Dr. Charles Owiredu for the Biblical Hebrew and Greek exegesis during our conversations, Blake Atwood for the initial editorial work on the manuscript, Emefa and her team - Charismata Edit Services for proofing and final editing and Francis Nsiah for the cover design.

To teachers, pastors, and mentors who I have been privileged to have throughout my younger years and now.

Blessings evermore!

Foreword

In this concise book, Nana Kwabena Anyani-Boadum applies the Pygmalion effect, to a larger extent, to help young people increase their general performance in any discipline they find themselves. Nana, like any responsible parent or teacher, has set some very high expectations for every child to reach their goal irrespective of their geographical location and the neighborhood in which they live. The writer believes that, notwithstanding your present disposition, there is so much you could accomplish if you accept the fact that there is a viable potential in you that is capable of making you the next world-changer if you put your mind to it.

There is an innate potential embedded within every human being but not until you come to the realization of the potential that lies deep within you and that the riches in your family cannot push you to ever reach the zenith of your life. The first step therefore is discovering just what that potential is. For some of you, this journey of self-awareness is an instinctive process, often helped by a watchful parent or teacher who spotted something in you from an early age and called it into being.

Most young people get stuck in life due to the spirit of doubt. Self-doubt is a potent weapon that has killed more dreams and visions than failure ever will. In this book, the writer talks about how most young people wrongly assume that successful people in the field of commerce, people in higher echelons of scientific research, or powerful preachers of the gospel of Christ, never had any doubts, were decisive about every choice they made, and never had regrets in the pursuit of their enterprise. But that couldn't be further from the truth. The fact is, everyone, even the most sanguine leaders, had doubts as they pursued their targets in life.

Self-doubt is a human response to the challenges life throws our way no matter the level of your spirituality or positivity. However, self-doubt should not stop anyone from overcoming obstacles and reaching his or her set goals.

All that the writer of this practical book is teaching is summed up in Hebrews 11:32–34:

"And what shall I more say? for the time would fail me to tell of Gideon, and of Barak, and of Samson, and of Jephthae; of David also, and Samuel, and of the prophets: Who through faith subdued kingdoms, wrought righteousness, obtained promises, stopped the mouths of lions. Quenched the violence of fire, escaped the edge of the sword, out of weakness were made strong, waxed valiant in fight, turned to flight the armies of the aliens."

The end line of verse 34 shows us that all those powerful guys, like Samson, David, and Jephthae, who subdued kingdoms and stopped the mouths of lions, were once very weak people who were made strong when they aligned their thoughts and spirits to God.

Nana Kwabena Anyani-Boadum loves children, and, since childhood, his passion has been to turn children who see themselves as "ordinary" into world-changers.

There are several classic books on children, but this is one of the most engaging that gives hope to every child. This book is a must-read for every young person with a curious mind.

Rt. Rev. Dr. Nana Anyani-Boadum
*Superintendent Bishop: Jesus Generation Ministries
*National Executive Member: Ghana Pentecostal and Charismatic Council
*Council Member: Regent University College of Science and Technology

Why I Wrote This Book

Growing up as a teenager and during my service as a young adults minister, one of the things I realized is that many children and young adults are amazed at the great things God does through people in all walks of life, whether in Christian ministry, in business management, or in commerce, etc. However, subtly and almost simultaneously, there is a wave of doubt, insecurity, and fear when we reflect on *our* potential to be used by God. Without the right guidance, encouragement, and love, many young people tend to conclude that they are not worthy or eligible for God to use them. Not only is that thought inaccurate, it is toxic and can prevent us from realizing God's purpose for our lives.

The goal of this book is to encourage young people to believe that God wants to and does use "ordinary" people to do great things for His purpose. It challenges the reader to shift their focus from their weaknesses and allow God to work in and through them. It references Bible characters whom God used and points to some of their own shortcomings, not in a demeaning manner, but as a way of inspiring hope in the reader.

It is my prayer that insights in this book will cause a shift in your thinking and give you a new revelation of God's love for you. You will be fully prepared to live a life that honors God and blesses the people around you.

God can and wants to use you!

Can God Use Me?

Many children and young people respect and have high expectations for the kinds of people God uses. They hold Bible characters, the men and women of God, and the spiritual movers and shakers of our world today in high esteem. However, this perception is not only restricted to religious achievers but also extends to sociopolitical and other sectors of society.

Generally, we highly esteem people with a status or position of authority and influence. In most cultures, people who have earned or received a prefix or suffix to their names are seen as powerful (e.g., professors, doctors, engineers, archbishops, reverends, etc.). The sense of awe and reverence accorded to them, and the towering achievements that accompany the mention of their names, almost give them a heroic recognition.

The antithesis to this is the inadequacy, incompetence, and frailty most young people sense when they see themselves as ordinary persons and, from afar, view the man or woman God uses as somewhat of an extraordinary being. One may begin to think lowly of him/herself and perceive the people God uses to be special super-beings. I believe this feeling becomes the bedrock on which the mind begins to ponder, *Can God use me?*

Although the accomplishments and notability of the people God uses should serve as motivation in an ideal situation, three issues can cause us to drift into self-pity and outright discouragement, not believing we are also candidates for God to use: (1) we may have only a partial understanding of the workings of God in and through them, (2) we may not see the distinction between their humanity and the work of divinity, and (3) sometimes we may fail to fully comprehend and remember that they are still mortals who have achieved extraordinary feats.

The Bible recounts the stories of men who commanded the sea to part into two, commanded fire to come down from heaven, killed wild animals with their bare hands, fed one hundred men with twenty loaves, defeated an army of thousands with a few men, healed the sick, cast out demons, walked on water, and performed many great and supernatural feats.

The powerful achievements of the men and women of God during biblical eras and in our time are so gargantuan that a young mind may sometimes find it hard to believe that the natural things that pertain to them, and every human being, for that matter, also apply to the people God uses. Humorously, these minds sometimes ask what may seem like dumb questions regarding the humanness of the people God uses. Among others, they may ask, "Do they use the washroom every morning like I do?" Or they ask, "What type of food do they eat?" Juxtaposing the greatness of the people God uses to the commonness of the young person is almost pitting the supernatural against the natural, and a grave disconnect is created between the two. So, they wonder and question, mostly subconsciously, *Can God use me as He uses others?*

Reflections

(After reading this chapter journal your thoughts or action plan)

Look at Some
People God Used

Let's take a walk down biblical memory lane and review some key characters God used greatly. The testimony and record of the accomplishments these Bible heroes wrought are worth showcasing. In this chapter, we'll look at the highlights of their ministries. These people were used greatly by God and just as we do with the men and women of God in our time, we will admire, read, and talk about these vessels of God from afar.

Besides only sharing the popular and glamorous headline facts we know about some of the people God used, I'll intersperse their stories with glimpses of their weaknesses in character or in action, sometimes shown through fear, low self-esteem, pride, lack of confidence, or, at other times, sheer craziness, even at critical moments of their ministries. The very traits you may sometimes exhibit that make you feel disqualified to be used by God for anything of significance are seen in the lives of these great people, even at the height of their ministries.

Moses

When a new king, Pharaoh, arose in the history of the Israelites who did not know Joseph, this king envisioned that the people of God would become mightier than the Egyptians. He thought that in a time of war, the Hebrews would side with the enemy faction and defeat the Egyptians and thus Pharaoh saw them as a threat. So his plan was to set taskmasters over the Israelites, torment them, and make their lives bitter with hard labor. But that was not all. He charged the head Hebrew midwives to annihilate all male-born children of the Israelites. His goal was to render the people of God powerless, rob them of any dream of rulership, and make them perpetual slaves. But a promise of deliverance hung on the lives of God's people, and one man was needed to bring it to pass. This is where Moses came on the scene, drawn out by God, to stand in the leadership gap.

This great man of God had the privilege of partnering with God in leading the people of God (Israel) out from over four hundred years of bondage in the "Operation Exodus to the Promised Land." The purpose of God delivered Moses from execution during his birth until the time of maturity, when he embraced his life's assignment. As a prequel and a sequel to the deliverance of the Israelites, God wrought many miracles by the hand of Moses as a grown man. Moses is a general in the kingdom of God by all standards, and one God used.

Let's take a look at some of the facts on his resume:

- Author of the first five books of the Holy Bible and possibly a few other books in the Old Testament

- Adopted son of Pharaoh's daughter, making him heir to the throne of Egypt (Exodus 2:5-10)
- God's agent in delivering the nation of Israel out of slavery in Egypt (Exodus 3:7-10)
- The only man God spoke to face-to-face (Exodus 33:11)
- Recipient of the Ten Commandments on tablets from God on Mount Sinai (Exodus 19, 20)
- Built the tabernacle of God (Exodus 31)
- Performed many miracles, such as turning water bodies into blood and causing frogs, lice, and flies to cover the face of the earth, which were among the many plagues he initiated to break Pharaoh's stubbornness and release God's people (Exodus 7 – 11)
- Parting the sea into two for the Israelites to walk on the seabed—a landmark miracle worth standing on its own (Exodus 14:21-27)
- The meekest man on the earth (Numbers 12:3)
- Over fifteen hundred years after his death, appears with Elijah, talking with Jesus at his transfiguration (Matthew 17:1–13)

What achievements for one man, unparalleled in all of history! Moses indeed is an example of the people God uses, and he is a special one in a class of his own. Moses is a legend par excellence.

Before you start highlighting your flaws to discredit your candidacy as a person God can also use, I want you to know that Moses, with all this greatness, had his weaknesses too. At the time of his call, he was probably the only servant of God who never wanted to embrace his assignment. He had a bag full of excuses and was unwilling to take that first step.

You may have acted that way before, or you may know someone who has. Although he was a fully grown man at the time of his call, Moses acted like a child. He tossed God back and forth more than ten times in his bid to escape the assignment he was born for (Exodus 3–4). He gave excuse upon excuse while God gave reason upon reason to counteract Moses's fears and justify his calling. But Moses kept shirking his responsibility.

He said things like, "I am nobody. How can I go to the king and bring the Israelites out of Egypt?" (Exodus 3:11). He questioned God's plan: "But suppose the Israelites do not believe me and will not listen to what I say. What shall I do if they say that you did not appear to me?" (Exodus 4:1). God answers by performing many miracles, including causing Moses's hand to turn leprous and healing it right after.

But the eighty-year-old man still did not have confidence in himself, and he remained afraid, he doubted God's ability, and he simply did not want to seize the moment of his call. Rather, he kept giving excuses: "No, Lord, don't send me. I have never been a good speaker … No, Lord, please send someone else" (Exodus 4:10, 4:13). This went on for quite some time until God eventually lost his cool and gave Moses an aide for the mission with full assurance of His presence:

> At this the Lord became angry with Moses and said, "What about your brother Aaron, the Levite? I know that he can speak well. In fact, he is now coming to meet you and will be glad to see you. You can speak to him and tell him what to say. I will help both of you to speak, and I will tell you both what to do. He will be your spokesman and speak to the people for you. Then you will be like

God, telling him what to say. Take this walking stick with you; for with it you will perform miracles." (Exodus 4:14–17 GNT)

Maybe accepting responsibility and standing up to do what you must do, or what you believe you are called to do, is your greatest weakness and challenge. You do not have the desire to take the initiative. You have become an excuse giver and are gradually losing confidence in yourself and your abilities.

Your story isn't exceptional, but neither is it hopeless. However, you must not remain apathetic. Don't give up. Lift your head up and let us begin to pick up the pieces, knowing that the people God used and uses have their weaknesses too, as we saw in Moses's life. Although he had his weaknesses, God used him in the end.

You are no different, my dear. God can use you!

Elijah

Let's take a quick look at another person God used: the man who appears to Jesus together with Moses at Jesus's transfiguration in Matthew 17 (Moses and Elijah symbolized the Law and the Prophets respectively). Indeed, for these men to be privileged to appear with Christ here is a great achievement never to be paralleled.

Elijah's record is also fascinating: he is the captain of the team of biblical prophets, a man often found in the deserts and wilderness. Although he didn't have the kind of upbringing Moses had, with all the pleasures of being brought up in the courts of royalty, Elijah still had a profound impact on Israel as a great prophet of God. In fact, many Bible scholars assert that Elijah is not yet dead; rather, he's still alive in his bodily form because he was taken up to heaven by God in a whirlwind without seeing death (2 Kings 2:1–14). In Revelation 11:1–14, the Bible talks about the two witnesses who will appear at the very end of our age. They are the two lampstands standing before the God of the earth and will perform many mighty wonders. In my opinion, based on research, Elijah will be one of the two witnesses, considering how his life and ministry parallels in every sense with the account in Revelations 11.

The fact that chariots of fire came through a whirlwind to whisk him away is not the only outstanding story about this great man of God. Besides the mass manna from heaven which fed all the Israelites, Elijah was probably the first man to be fed out of heaven's kitchen. By a raven, he received a full-course meal twice a day. Wow! At other times, he was fed by an angel (1 Kings 17:2–4; 19:5–6).

Elijah prays for a widow's meal and oil to be multiplied for many days. He prays for a dead boy to be raised back to life. He challenges over 450 prophets in a conquest to know who serves the one true God, and he calls fire from heaven to consume his sacrifice. What a man! In fact, it would not be an exaggeration to say, 'what a *superman!*'

Indeed, Elijah is another example of the people God uses, but he had his weaknesses too. At one point in his ministry, he switches from bragging about being God's last bet against the enemies (1 Kings 18:22) to a low point of discouragement after enduring the stressful ordeal of running away from Jezebel, the woman who sought his life (1 Kings 19:4).

Listen to the narrative of a man of God who felt like a failure and whose moods swung like a pendulum. "I have had enough,

Lord," he says. "Take my life, for I am no better than my ancestors who have already died" (1 Kings 19:4). Those are the words of a depressed and dejected man who wanted to end it all. The overwhelming attacks and challenges he faced during this period of his ministry made him contemplate *suicide*.

> "When you feel down or overwhelmed by many challenges, when thoughts of giving up come to you, it's nothing strange, but it must not be permitted to stay with you."

My dear friend, I'm talking about a man whom God used greatly. He was at his wit's end, or so he thought. You see, when you feel down or overwhelmed by many challenges, when thoughts of giving up come to you, it's nothing strange, but it must not be permitted to stay with you. God has a better plan that guarantees your stability and peace even amid your weaknesses and fears. It's called *grace*, and He has freely made it available to us.

Your weaknesses do not exempt you from God's plan. He is passionate about working with your limitations and doing great things through you.

Jeremiah

Jeremiah, who even has an entire book of the Bible named after him, is another general God used mightily. He spoke strongly on backsliding and the judgment that God's people face when they become apostates. His ministry was significant to the final gathering of Israel after many years of captivity. After Israel had enjoyed the goodness of God for several centuries they made some grievous choices. God had given them economic victories, battle victories, territorial victories, financial victories and the likes.

However, they forgot the God that delivered them from the Egyptian bondage and pursued idolatry. This act, led them into Babylonian captivity for seventy years. And while there, it was through the prophet Jeremiah that God initiated their deliverance. By sending His word to Jeremiah, the prophet spoke comforting words to the Israelites in bondage. He prophesied to them saying, "For I know the thoughts that I think toward you, says the Lord, thoughts of peace and not of evil, to give you a future and a hope."

Yet, this great prophet had his weaknesses too. At the time of his call, Brother Jeremiah didn't think he was up to the task and looked down upon himself because he was a youth. For that matter, he thought nothing great could be done with him or through him.

> "'O Sovereign Lord,' I said, 'I can't speak for you!
> I'm too young!' The Lord replied, 'Don't say, "I'm
> too young," for you must go wherever I send you
> and say whatever I tell you.'"
>
> Jeremiah 1:6–7 NLT

The Apostle Paul's admonishment to his spiritual son Timothy would have been handy to Jeremiah in this case:

> "Don't let anyone think less of you because you are
> young. Be an example to all believers in what you
> say, in the way you live, in your love, your faith,
> and your purity."

1 Timothy 4:12 NLT

How many young people haven't shunned the call of God to do something great, many times citing similar reasons as Jeremiah? It may be a desire that has long been in your heart to do something unique, a desire that sometimes feels strange, but you know it's like a special assignment. It may be to start a small Bible study group, start an awareness campaign to address certain vices in society, develop that hobby into a business, develop that creative mobile app, write a novel, or do whatever you feel led in your heart to do.

My dear friend, you are not too young. God can use you.

Gideon

This man is a member of the faith hall of fame for by his hand were mighty miracles done. Leading an army of only three hundred men, Gideon successfully annihilated the Midianites. But he had to learn to trust God first.

> "And the Angel of the Lord appeared to him, and said to him, 'The Lord is with you, you mighty man of valor!' Gideon said to Him, 'O my lord, if the Lord is with us, why then has all this happened to us? And where are all His miracles which our fathers told us about, saying, "Did not the Lord bring us up from Egypt?" But now the Lord has forsaken us and delivered us into the hands of the Midianites.' Then the Lord turned to him and said, 'Go in this might of yours, and you shall save Israel from the hand of the Midianites. Have I not

sent you?' So, he said to Him, 'O my Lord, how
can I save Israel? Indeed, my clan is the weakest
in Manasseh, and I am the least in my father's
house.' And the Lord said to him, 'Surely I will be
with you, and you shall defeat the Midianites as
one man.'"

Judges 6:12–16

When the Angel of the Lord came to him and addressed him as
God saw him, as a "mighty man of valor" (Judges 6:12), Gideon
quickly retorted and described himself as nobody, a weakling, and
the least in his clan: "I am the least in my father's house" (Judges
6:15). He doubted whether God was truly with them and was
unsure if he could bank his hopes on Him: "O my lord, if the Lord
is with us, why then has all this happened to us?" (Judges 6:13).

Gideon did not count himself as part of the solution of bringing
deliverance to God's people, but God had planned it to be done
through him. Even when God encouraged Gideon to take a step
of faith because He was the one sending him, Gideon went on to
remind God of his own nativity and how insignificant his people
were: "Indeed my clan is the weakest in Manasseh" (Judges 6:15).

Does this sound like you? When God somehow led you to an
opportunity in life or a challenge that required you to stretch
yourself in all ways, have you ever looked back at your nativity and
family history? Do you easily throw in the towel at such moments,
giving the excuse that you're not competent enough to handle it
or that someone else deserves it and not you?

You may be expecting some form of blessing or opportunity, but
what may come at you is a task that needs to be done and its

reward may lead to that blessing you desire. But will you have the courage to take on that task, learn to tackle it, solve the mystery, and reap the rewards? Or will you look down on yourself and just give up, blaming God for not answering your prayer or for forsaking you?

> *"You will never know what you are capable of until you step out in faith."*

Know this: you will never know what you are capable of until you step out in faith, take your chances, and give that challenge a try. In doing that, you will realize that God is with you at each moment. But sitting idle and thinking God's presence will do the work does not solve the problem. God desires to work it out *with* you, but He needs you to take the first step in faith.

Can you imagine what would have happened if Gideon had never stepped out in faith and obedience because he thought his three-hundred-man army was too small to do anything great for God? But when he did, God worked a miracle through that and Gideon is recorded in history as a man who also walked by faith.

Gideon was truly another general God used to do mighty things, but he had his weaknesses too.

The Twelve Disciples of Jesus

The twelve disciples were Simon Peter, Andrew, James, John, Philip, Bartholomew (Nathanael), Thomas, Matthew, James the Less,

Lebbaeus (Judas; Thaddaeus), Simon (Zealot) and Judas Iscariot. These men are also a unique group of people; specially handpicked by the greatest teacher of all time who mentored them for three-and-a-half years after which, the ministry of their master was entrusted to their charge. They were young adults, most likely in their twenties, except for Peter, who may have been in his thirties. They preached, healed the sick, and prayed for the restoration of sight to the blind, for the lame to walk, and for the deaf to hear and thus performed countless miracles.

The church is what it is today because these men sacrificed, loyally served, stood their ground, and led the crusade that kept the torch burning as they passed it on to the next generation of church leaders. In fact, their accomplishments transcend into eternity, for their names will be inscribed on the foundation of the New Jerusalem according to Revelation 21:14. Wow!

But they had their imperfections and weaknesses too.

We read in Scripture several times about how they battled for attention and competed among themselves as to who was most influential, powerful, and worthy to be the leader of the group (Matthew 18:1 – 5, Luke 9:46 – 48, Mark 9:33 -37). Just like many of us crave to be in the spotlight, they all wanted prominence, status, and attention, and they argued about this. They were mostly selfish.

With different temperaments on display and some possibly holding divergent ideological and political views, the master mentor Jesus took them through a three-and-a-half-year personal training session with the aim to birth a spirit of oneness in them and make them fit for His use. In John 17:22, Jesus prayed "that they may be one."

Have you ever been fearful at something or ever dozed off during a prayer meeting? During one voyage on the Sea of Galilee, the disciples shivered to the spine when a violent storm arose. On another occasion, when the master walked on water, they were so terrified that they thought they had seen a ghost. When the Master asked them to pray with Him through the night in the Garden of Gethsemane before his crucifixion, they could not do so for even an hour and they fell asleep.

Have you raised your eyebrows when someone gave a huge offering at church, thinking to yourself what the money would be used for? Or have you doubted the power of prayer even after praying or after a prayer was said for you? Such was the case with the disciples. At one point, one of them questioned a woman for offering an expensive perfume to Jesus, breaking it, and then anointing Him with it. They thought there could be a better use for that perfume when sold and given to the poor. They were slow to grasp their master's teachings, acted irrationally several times, doubted the power of God to cast out demons, and even failed at some of the missions they were sent on.

To build a winning and successful team out of the twelve men could easily be labeled as "Mission Impossible," but I AM made it possible! Unstable Simon was transformed into a rock. The son of thunder, John, who at one point called for an entire town and people to be burned down, would become the Apostle of love. Their long-held traditions would be challenged by the faith and power of Jesus. Parable after parable, lesson after lesson, miracle after miracle, these imperfect men handpicked by Jesus would be transformed into useful tools in the hands of God.

Slowly but surely, they became teachable and were receptive to their master's voice.

The Apostle Paul

Saul of Tarsus was a revered man within Jerusalem's circles of influence during his day. An astute learner of the Law of Moses, he studied under some of the most distinguished and erudite rabbis, such as Gamaliel. Before Jesus Christ converted him, Saul was a radical persecutor of the early disciples of Jesus and His church. The Church and her leadership feared Saul, as he would go to the extremes of taking orders and arresting all "people of the Way", as the early Christians were known. He would also imprison both males *and* females (Acts 8:3).

> "From persecutor to preacher and murderer to missionary, God picked a man like Saul despite his background and used him for His glory."

The Bible records that Saul was present at the stoning of Stephen, who became the first Christian martyr and Saul was the custodian of the garments of Stephen's executioners (Acts 7:58). Saul hated the believers (Christians) with every fiber of his being, and his zeal to exterminate them seemed to never diminish. No one could stop Saul—until a fateful day on the Damascus road.

As Saul went on his way to extradite Christians back to Jerusalem, the persecutor was arrested by the very person he tormented: Jesus Christ (Acts 9:3–9; 22:6–11; 26:12–18). The resurrected Jesus appeared in a great light to Saul and this caused Saul to be struck with blindness. After three days, God sent Ananias of Damascus to pray for the restoration of Saul's sight. **After being struck by The Great Light, Saul became a light-bearer himself.** He was transformed from a fervent tormentor of Christians to one of Christianity's greatest proponents.

Later to be called Paul the Apostle, this man was not one of the twelve apostles Jesus chose but he is undoubtedly a pillar of the New Testament church and a great servant and missionary of God. He was primarily the Apostle to the Gentiles, but, taking advantage of his background as both a Jew and a Roman citizen, he ministered extensively to both people groups. From persecutor to preacher and murderer to missionary, God picked a man like Saul despite his background and used him for His glory.

The history of the apostle Paul as a callous, vivacious, cruel, and abrasive murderer paints a picture of a bold and high-spirited personality. After his conversion, we tend to think such a person would always be on fire, confident, daring, and actively going about his dealings. We think of Paul as an outspoken person and a powerful orator, and we perceive him as one with exceptional speaking skills.

But he was not always in high spirits and ever-ready to do life and ministry. He was not always as confident and bold as we may think he was. People are not always what they appear to be. In fact, Paul relied fully on God and did not consider his outward appearance or physical effort, which was scorned by many.

"I know that someone is saying that my letters are powerful and strong, but that I'm a weakling and a terrible speaker."

2 Corinthians 10:10 GW

He was fearful many times. He was not always strong and zealous as it may seem; he lived in and through moments of fear, depression, weakness, and torture. However, those moments or attributes did not define him neither did they deny him the opportunity to be a part of the great move of God during his generation.

Here, we see God encouraging him to step out and continue the work of speaking and preaching at a moment when fear might have gripped him:

"Now the Lord spoke to Paul in the night by a vision, 'Do not be afraid, but speak, and do not keep silent.'"

Acts 18:9

Your countenance may not look impressive. You may not have the ideal height, body shape, voice, or what have you, but look at Paul. Your seemingly negative attributes of fear, weakness, and timidity should not disqualify you from being used by God. Paul may not have been as eloquent as we perceive him, and he was not always bold and daring. He sometimes ministered out of fear and weakness. He was not dependent on himself; rather, he relied on God's strength and grace.

If you do the same, God can use you. The people God used also felt inadequate. If you think or feel that you're not good enough, not important enough, not a good speaker, or wonder what you can say or do for God, remember this: It's not about you. It's about God, and He will use you for His glory.

> "Not that we are sufficient of ourselves to think of anything as being from ourselves, but our sufficiency is from God."
>
> 2 Corinthians 3:5

It Is Not By Might

We could talk about others like David, Abraham, Ruth, Jabez and more and how God used them to do great things, but in highlighting the humanness and frailties of Elijah, Jeremiah, Gideon, the disciples, and Paul, I desire to inspire hope and drag us out of the gutter of self-pity, apathy, little thinking, fear, and discouragement, so we might step out into the light of God's glorious purpose for each of us.

Just like the generals we read of in the Bible, today's servants of God are ordinary human beings. Despite their resounding feats of success, massive crusade gatherings, multi-million-dollar humanitarian projects, marvelous worship experiences, and immense church buildings, all of which have given them an unapproachable superman status, these generals of God have their share of limitations and weaknesses too. However, they possess a unique ability, "the anointing," to perform and achieve outstanding results in their ministries and within their church circles.

When we experience supernatural encounters accomplished by a natural human, or when God uses ordinary people to accomplish great feats, we say they are *anointed* for such causes. The anointing is an unction to function, and God graciously gives men this ability to achieve heaven's will in the earthly realm. The anointing gives people a unique ability to do great or difficult tasks with ease.

> "It shall come to pass in that day that his burden will be taken away from your shoulder, And his yoke from your neck, And the yoke will be destroyed because of the anointing oil"
>
> Isaiah 10:27

The anointing produces miracles, breaks the bondage of demonic oppression, restores peace to families, gives the wisdom to build healthy and loving homes, build houses, structures, and edifices, run profitable businesses and ministries, and judiciously manage our affairs. The anointing endows different people with special gifts to function in different areas of ministry and administration. It is such a sweet and gracious influence.

> "There are diversities of gifts, but the same Spirit. There are differences of ministries, but the same Lord. And there are diversities of activities, but it is the same God who works all in all"
>
> 1 Corinthians 12:4–6

The anointing attracts and that is one reason why we are mostly struck with awe when we witness or experience what God does with the people He chooses.

Reflections

(After reading this chapter journal your thoughts or action plan)

The Anointed And
The Anointing

Although the anointing is striking and attractive, it can easily be scorned and abused. One reason some despise the anointing is the nature of the vessel in which the anointing operates. Do not despise the anointing!

You see, a brother can be so gentle, eloquent, and such a powerful preacher, but off the pulpit, he may be sly, quick-tempered, and uncouth. Someone may be gifted as a good manager and builder, and she or he may be an outstanding Christian businessperson, but out of the office, you encounter an ill-mannered personality. A sister can dress well, sing so powerfully, and minister prophetically in church, but backstage, she may be sharp-tongued, unkempt, and unpleasant.

Somehow, the sweetness of the anointing upon their lives is unable to permeate their stubborn natures and leaves a sour taste in the mouth of anyone who experiences this duality in the personality of the anointed one. This tempts some to look down on the anointing. At other times, people do not have any regard for God and because they do not have a good understanding of the workings of the Holy Spirit, they disdain the anointing and the anointed. Such persons are to be wary.

THE ANOINTING IS AWESOME, BUT CHARACTER IS CRITICAL

The anointing that operates in the people God uses is distinct from their human character and behavior. The former is mostly a gift that is given and works through us with ease, although it requires the recipient to remain connected to God through prayer and Bible study to grow more spiritually. The latter is that part of a person's personality that is formed based on individual upbringing styles and learning experiences from school, church, and life. This must be worked on to be socially acceptable and pleasing to God.

> **No matter the accomplishments or accolades we receive, we must consciously strive to develop Christ-like character. God expects this from all of us.**

God expects His every anointed servant to continuously work on themselves, in terms of their character, to conform to the image of His Son. And this expectation is not for only men or women of God in the teaching and preaching ministry; it is an expectation for all of us. To have a Christ-like character that is seen and shown through the fruit of the Spirit is one of God's purposes for our lives here on earth.

"But the fruit of the Spirit is love, joy, peace, longsuffering, kindness, goodness, faithfulness, gentleness, self-control. Against such things there is no law."

Galatians 5:22–23

Our prayer thus should always be for God to create in us a clean heart and renew a right spirit within us (Psalm 51:10), to help us to learn through the circumstances and experiences of life, and, by the help of His Holy Spirit, form the character of Christ in us. Remember, once you are born again, you have the enabling power of the Holy Spirit working in you. Having weaknesses does not disqualify you. Recognizing your frailty and giving yourself up for God's total use is all you need to do to embrace his strength in your areas of struggle.

Reflections

(After reading this chapter journal your thoughts or action plan)

See Yourself As God Sees You

Often, that poor, downtrodden image we may have of ourselves as inadequate, incapable, or untalented is very different from how God sees us. Knowing the very fiber of our being—we were created in God's image and likeness—God knows well that we are capable, powerful, and blessed beyond measure (Ephesians 1:3).

Begin to see yourself as God sees you. While God saw Gideon as a mighty man of valor, Gideon thought otherwise about himself. He described himself as a weakling and the least in his father's house (Judges 6:12, 15). While Saul of Tarsus, later to be called Paul, saw himself as a persecutor, killer, and tormentor, God saw him as an apostle, a church planter, and a builder of God's church and His people.

While your past may have left a bad self-image of who you are, you are not your past. God made you and knows who you are. While your place of birth or the circumstances surrounding your birth may have left a stigma on you, you are God's masterpiece, carefully created for good works. Your true image and identity are rooted in Christ Jesus.

Reject the Wrong Label

Whenever you go grocery shopping or stroll through the mall to window-shop, labels likely catch your attention. The label on a product informs consumers of the product's identity, essence, purpose, and sometimes worth. Labels create difference and give meaning. If you were looking for an infant meal for your little one and mistakenly picked up incorrectly labeled canned food meant for dogs, that could be catastrophic. Sometimes, even the wrong labeling of product shelves can lead to such grave mistakes. If you're not observant and diligent as a consumer, you may have a disaster at hand.

Very similar shoes could all be stacked on a rack, but each pair may have a different label. The label of a known, high-value brand, which has established its value over the years, is mostly imitated by cheap, fly-by-night competitors whose brand names may not be as well-known. However, the label on that high-end shoe qualifies it as a valuable product worth its price, whatever that price might be. The durability of these shoes may not vary much, but the brand name and label distinguish one pair of shoes from another.

With these examples, we see how labels can define a product and show its worth and purpose. In the same way, our self-portrait can be sketched from a label we have placed on ourselves based on our understanding of who we are or from a label society wrongly places on us. In this section, I would like to address those who have carved self-portraits based on a label placed on them by society. One fact of life is that people may never see any good in you, but out of jealousy, envy, or for no reason at all, they choose to define you by your shortcomings. If you find yourself in such a situation, this is my word to you: reject the wrong label!

Jesus, who knew who He was and the assignment on His life, did not mince words whenever He spoke of Himself as the Son of God, the Savior of mankind, and the work He came to earth to do (John 10:10; Luke 4:16–21).

But when people during Jesus's day, whether out of familiarity or jealousy, struggled to accept Him for who He says He was, wrestled with His teachings and doubted how He spoke with authority, they slighted him and wrongly labeled him.

> *"Is not this the carpenter's son?"*
>
> Matthew 13:55

By that passing comment, they sought to discredit Him, His origin, and His assignment. They sought to refute claims of His *messiahship* by saying, essentially, "We know who His parents are. We grew up with Him and played in the streets with Him. He's one of us, and there's nothing special about Him." In another instance, they even ascribed his power to demons, but Jesus, full of wisdom and knowledge of His identity, always had a way to handle such naysayers and distracters.

Observe how wrong labels were attached to some other key personalities in the Bible, as I believe is still the case for many today.

"Now Jephthah the Gileadite was a mighty man of valor, **but he was the son of a harlot**: and Gilead begot Jephthah."

Judges 11:1 (emphasis mine)

"Now Naaman, captain of the host of the king of Syria, was a great man with his master, and honourable, because by him the Lord had given deliverance unto Syria: he was also a mighty man in valour, **but he was a leper**."

2 Kings 5:1 KJV (emphasis mine)

People will use one little conjunction: *but*, and with that, they will showcase and catalog your shortcomings, inabilities, or unfortunate past life events. As if to undermine the outstanding track record of the great general Naaman, one little phrase, "he was a leper," introduced after the word *but*, would leave an indelible mark in every reader's mind. The only characteristic of Naaman you might remember after reading this verse is that he was a leper and *not* that he won many victories for Israel. How sad!

Today, we might say something like, "She's an outstanding student, *but* she's always wearing the same clothes. She's a great fashion designer, *but* she's a divorcee. He's an astute politician, *but* he's physically challenged. She's a great preacher, *but* she's a single mother." You may have a challenge, shortcoming, or an unfortunate past life event, but don't focus on the '*but*' in your life.

Reject the wrong label. Our weaknesses and limitations should not become an obstruction to create a huge barrier that prevents us from giving ourselves up for God to use.

Wrong labels are placed on people because of one circumstance or the other. Do not allow events and circumstances which you do not have control over (such as your place of birth, parentage, etc.) to be used as a label against you. Labels have the capacity to determine a person's ability, significance, use, and worth. Accepting the wrong label and living by it can thus rob you of your original purpose and the promises which God has given you.

> God can use you despite your buts.

Embrace the Truth

The antidote to this wrong label is constantly considering the mirror of God's Word. The Word of God tells us who we truly are in Christ Jesus and reveals the power that is available to us once we embrace our position as God's children by accepting Jesus as our Lord and personal Savior. Humbly studying the Word of God, joining and interacting with other believers who are also committed to Christ Jesus and His Word, and always talking to God (prayer) are the ways we discover who we truly are and gain the power to reject wrong labels.

Most of us may easily assert that we believe what the Good Book says and believe every word God speaks, but we hardly make time to read it. We may have different inhibitors, but I think if we decide to manage our media consumption appropriately and apportion our time well, we can get better in this area. Pastor Rick Warren once posted this quote to Facebook:

"If you want to get wiser, spend less time on Facebook and more time with your face in The Book."[1]

Embrace the truth of God's Word in 1 Peter 2:9. It is yours. Recite it, mutter it, and make it your confession. Believe it, receive it, and declare, "It's mine!"

"But you are a chosen race, a royal priesthood, a holy nation, a people for His own possession, that you may proclaim the excellencies of Him who called you out of darkness into His marvelous light."

1 Peter 2:9 ESV

Grace for Guilt

One of the main reasons we do not see ourselves as God sees us is guilt. God created us and owns us and we are accountable to Him. One day, we will all stand before the throne of God to give an account of our lives (Romans 14:12; Hebrews 4:13; 1 Peter 4:5). So, our focus in life must be to please Him.

But when we switch God's role in our lives and decide to please other people or ourselves, we end up doing the very things that God does not recommend for us. We miss the mark He has set for us, and we end up in sin. That feeling of guilt, which also births fear, draws us away from God and keeps us from allowing God to use us.

Sin causes us to focus on our weaknesses instead of His grace and forgiveness. Our minds become clouded with all our wrongdoings to the extent that the thought of God using us to accomplish anything significant is deemed impossible and far beyond us. **We feel unqualified for the Master's use because of guilt, which results from sin.** We are held down by guilt and condemnation and an unwillingness to allow God to use us. But I have good news for you.

When we acknowledge our sins and accept God's forgiveness and grace to turn around for better and are baptized in Jesus' name, He truly wipes away our sin and gives us hope for a brighter tomorrow. Everyone can enjoy this grace of God because of the work of His Son Jesus Christ on the cross many years ago. Accept His grace.

> "Having wiped out the handwriting of requirements that was against us, which was contrary to us. And He has taken it out of the way, having nailed it to the cross."
>
> Colossians 2:14

When we sin and get caught in that feeling of guilt, we feel forsaken by God and tend to think that by doing certain good deeds, we can regain His affection and love. As much as God expects good deeds from us, the notion of performing some deeds to merit His love is misplaced. Any act of service that is not first rooted in love does not please God, and God being love Himself first shows us love and enables us to love back also:

> "But God demonstrates His own love toward us, in that while we were still sinners, Christ died for us."
>
> Romans 5:8

You are loved by God, and this love is our motivation for obeying God's laws. Our obedience also then becomes a measure of our love for God. The Bible puts it this way:

> "Now by this we know that we know Him, if we keep His commandments ... But whoever keeps His word, truly the love of God is perfected in him. By this we know that we are in Him."

> 1 John 2:3, 5

See yourself as God's beloved child. See yourself as one completely forgiven. See yourself as one filled with the Holy Ghost. See yourself as one who has God's backing and help to accomplish every task. See yourself as capable and custom-made by God for a specific assignment.

Reflections

(After reading this chapter journal your thoughts or action plan)

Children: At The Heart Of The Father

"Behold, children are a heritage from the Lord,
The fruit of the womb is a reward."

Psalm 127:3

Dear parent or guardian, your child is a gift from God. You get to become custodians of this precious gift during their lifetime here on earth. This is both a responsibility and a privilege and God expects you to care for the children with utmost love and devotion.

The attention and care we normally give to things we cherish and hold dear shows how valuable they are to us. What if you received precious jewelry as a gift, or purchased a new smartphone you saved money to buy or bought that new dress? Obviously, you wouldn't leave that fine jewelry on the kitchen table, or leave that new smartphone to on the floor to be trampled on by people, or wear that new dress as your pajamas. These are just things, but we do not handle them roughly because we treasure them.

If we treat the things we really like with gentleness, then we must have a higher standard when dealing with people. We must treat the people we love with honor. Children are special gifts from God and because of how fragile and innocent they are, we must treat them with the utmost love, care and respect. They have a special place in God's heart.

> "Take heed that you do not despise one of these little ones, for I say to you that in heaven their angels always see the face of My Father who is in heaven."
>
> Matthew 18:10

All children have angels, and these angels are in what I call those in the "VIP lounge of God's presence." They have access to God's presence and always behold his face. Children are special, likable, and lovely, and God holds them very dearly. God expects parents, guardians, teachers and older people with the responsibility of caring for children, to do so with gladness and love. God does not approve of any act of neglect or abuse targeted at these little ones. Children are defenseless, and need leadership. We must protect them, comfort them, teach them the truth and guide them towards their God-given destiny.

> "But whoever causes one of these little ones who believe in Me to sin, it would be better for him if a millstone were hung around his neck, and he were drowned in the depth of the sea."
>
> Matthew 18:6

Dear parent or guardian, you have big shoes to fill. Are you ready? Our Heavenly Father's love for His children is unquestionable.

We see the heart of God when it comes to his love for children through the life of Jesus. The Bible makes it clear that while on earth, Jesus Christ said and did nothing except what His Father told Him to do. In His actions, we see the heartbeat and desire of God Almighty. All Jesus did was what God would have done.

> "For I did not speak on my own, but the Father who sent me commanded me to say all that I have spoken."
>
> John 12:49 NIV

> "Jesus gave them this answer: "Very truly I tell you, the Son can do nothing by himself; he can do only what he sees his Father doing, because whatever the Father does the Son also does."
>
> John 5:19 NIV

In the pages of Scripture, we see Jesus carrying little children on His lap, gently talking to them, and loving and praying for them. We hear Him metaphorically using children and the disposition of their hearts as the standard of acceptance into His Father's kingdom. He said things like, "unless you are converted and become like children, you will not enter the kingdom of heaven" (Matthew 18:3). Here, "little child" is *paidion* in Greek, and it refers to a child under the age of seven.[2] We hear Jesus talk about the childlike faith we need if we are going to attract God's attention and achieve great things in life.

Little children are easy to convince. Adults think children believe every lie. On the other hand, adults are difficult to convince. They seem to know a lot, and that knowledge makes them analyze and scrutinize everything presented to them before accepting it. Although that isn't bad in itself, in matters of faith, this "intelligence" becomes foolishness, and the child's "naïveté" makes him a winner because he humbly believes and wholeheartedly accepts the truth of God's Word.

> "Assuredly, I say to you, whoever does not receive the kingdom of God as a little child will by no means enter it."
>
> Mark 10:15

Jesus truly showed that children mean a lot to God through His relationship with them while on earth. They were a key feature of his utterances, and we must not take this for granted as some do. A case in point occurred when the disciples, acting quite similar to some present-day church ushering team members, restricted little children from coming close to see Jesus for fellowship and prayer (Mark 10:13 – 16, Matthew 19:13 – 15). Jesus, unlike some of today's celebrity preachers, did not find this very amusing. He was very displeased. In fact, some have said that He was angrier at this scene than he was when he chanced upon people trading in the temple courts and switched to "Jet Li" mode, chasing out the money changers with whips.

Let us do an exegesis of the text in Mark 10.

> "Then they brought little children to Him, that He might touch them; but the disciples rebuked those who brought them. But when Jesus saw it, He was greatly displeased…"
>
> Mark 10:13 – 14

Eganaktesen is the Greek rendition of the word used to describe Jesus's mood and reaction in this text. It is one of the strongest used in all the New Testament. It is the past tense of the word *Aganakteo,* which is derived from two Greek words – *agan* (much) and *akhthomai* (grief or pain). This word *aganakteo* describes excessive pain and displeasure. It is intense pain or a feeling of shock aroused by injustice. Some also translate *aganakteo* as indignation. Anger aroused by an undignifying, unfair, mean or disgusting act.

Jesus was shocked at the action of His disciples. These children are defenseless, denying them access to Jesus was an act of injustice that displeased and caused Him excessive pain.

Dear parent or guardian, how do you react when children are unfairly treated? Do you recognize it when a child or vulnerable person is denied some benefits? Denying children access to good nutrition, healthcare, quality education are all acts of injustice that greatly afflicts God. Will you stand in the place of Jesus today to 'fight' against malnutrition, physical torture, child labor, child trafficking and other vices that plague our society? Do not leave this 'fight' to government, big corporations or the church.

To my dear little child or young adult, you have every right to come to Jesus. You are valuable to God. Be excited about it. He loves you and calls you His own. One thing we seem to forget is that unlike the first Adam, who was a full adult when he was created, Jesus was born of a virgin and grew from a baby into adulthood. At one point, Jesus was a little child also. He knows just how special children are and how essential that period of life is to our development and life's purpose.

Jesus, the Seventh-Grader

Dear young person, I want you to understand that God has a plan for your life and as long as you are alive—it doesn't matter your age—He wants to use you to fulfill a great purpose on earth. Even younger ones must be more encouraged and determined to discover and live out their God-ordained purposes now and not when they have a master's degree, or are married and working, or are suffering from midlife crises. God wants to use you today, even as a child or young adult, and that is why He set the example with His own Son, Jesus, even as a young child.

If Jesus were enrolled in a public or private school in your community, He would be in the seventh grade by the time we read of Him sitting in the temple courts, listening and asking the teachers of the law (i.e., rabbis), lawyers, and professors of his day questions on different aspects of the Torah (Luke 2:41–50).

The wisdom and confidence a "seventh-grade Jesus" showed while discussing the Scriptures in the temple were not a magical phenomenon. He grew in wisdom and into maturity through continual fellowship and communion with the Holy Spirit and other human teachers (Isaiah 50:4; Psalm 119:97–104). In the Messianic scripture of Isaiah, we see how the Holy Spirit Himself daily trained Jesus from childhood even though He had been filled with the Holy Spirit from birth.

You too can attain this all-around growth, and the sure way to start is to set a special time aside, preferably each dawn, where you read God's Word, pray, and commune with the Holy Spirit. Irrespective of your age, once you develop this routine and become committed to it, the master teacher, God's Holy Spirit, will impart wisdom to you, which will make you victorious in all things. That is how God prepares and equips the people He uses.

> "And the Child grew and became strong in spirit, filled with wisdom; and the grace of God was upon Him."
>
> Luke 2:40

> "And Jesus increased in wisdom and stature, and in favor with God and men."
>
> Luke 2:52

That is holistic growth. Jesus had his quiet time often, so the Holy Spirit taught Him deep things and gave Him profound wisdom. I recall some fond memories from my days at Scripture Union camps, where we were taught and made to practice our quiet times (or Morning devotions) daily. We even learned a nice song about quiet times and that is my admonishment to you, dear reader:

"A quiet time is the secret of a Christian daily life. Abraham did it, David observed it, Jesus had his quiet time often. So don't miss it, so, so don't miss it."

Don't Underestimate Them

Children and young people, do not underestimate your potential as a child of God. Give yourself daily to a quiet time of prayer and Bible study and maintain your fellowship with other believers. God will use you greatly!

Parents and guardians, do not keep singing that chorus of "Oh, they are too little / This is too much for them / Just take your time with them" when it comes to doing anything that has the potential to deepen their relationship with God through Jesus Christ. Have you wondered why you never assumed such a posture of "oh, they are too little" when it comes to kids expressing their talents or passions in other forms, like dancing to secular music, reading for long hours in preparation for final exams, or misconducting themselves in public through vulgar discourse? But you may believe that memorizing fifty scriptures is too much for your six-year-old, or reading through the entire Bible is impossible for your twelve-year-old, or leading the next worship service at church isn't doable for your teenager. Renew your mind through the washing of the Word!

Although it has been said that life begins at forty, in God's plan, Jesus had to finish His assignment on earth as a young adult at thirty-three years old. My dear friend, little child, or young adult, step out in faith and live the purpose of God for your life now in a way that honors God. How well you live this part of your life on earth has eternal implications on how you will live the next life. Life has begun; live it!

Don't Send Them Away

God loves children and young people so much, but the adults responsible for their training, care, and upbringing do not always exemplify this welcoming nature and character of love. A child's or young adult's confidence in themselves is greatly hampered by the type of reception they are accorded when in the company of older people whether at home, school, church, or in any place they find themselves.

Sadly, today, some adults have a general notion that children are troublesome and cannot be part of anything organized and meaningful. Although children can be a handful to deal with, they must not be treated as insignificant and a pain to deal with. The Bible says they are a blessing from God and guess what, apart from Adam and Eve, all of us had a childhood!

For those who see children and teens as troublemakers, they are unable to receive their presence and involvement as a blessing. The slightest chance to part ways with these little "insignificant" ones is such a relief to these adults. You can easily tell from the sudden expression of joy and happiness when kids are dropped off at school, or how some of them push them to the children's church as they are on their way to the "main" church service. In fact, many church ministries sadly ignore the children and do not seem to prioritize them. We can tell this by looking at the budget allocation for church activities, programs, and projects within the ministry. The attention given by top-level leadership to the operations of the children's ministry, the love, care, and appreciation given to these children to make them feel a part of the entire ministry, and the general concern and involvement leaders show toward the children. The picture painted in some of these unfortunate situations is not so different from the attitude of the disciples of Jesus when little children wanted to come into Jesus's church to also feel loved.

I strongly believe that when parents, families, churches, and nations focus on the welfare of children and teens, God will greatly bless them.

Speak Kindly To Them

"Death and life are in the power of the tongue, and those who love it will eat its fruit."

Proverbs 21:18

The tongue has incredible power and every word we utter can build up or destroy people. Parents and guardians have the unique privilege of speaking into the lives of their children. Even babies can recognize sound in utero. By the second trimester of pregnancy (between the third to the sixth month), most babies start developing their sense of hearing. This gives every mother an excellent opportunity to begin shaping the life of their unborn child with words, an act that I believe must continue even as the child grows. This principle of declaring positive words kindly into the life of a child doesn't only end with expectant mothers. Even if one did not have the opportunity to personally carry a child in their womb, this life-molding act of ministering kindly to them can and must continue. This will help build up the children under such a person's care.

"Do not use harmful words, but only helpful words, the kind that build up and provide what is needed, so that what you say will do good to those who hear you."

Ephesians 4:29 GNT

There is a seed of greatness in every child or young person that must be watered with kind and encouraging words. Being able to notice little efforts and achievements of children, duly acknowledging, encouraging and providing reward systems for them, will help create a conducive climate to nurture the seed of greatness within them. Countless dreams and hopes have been shattered because a parent, guardian, coach or older sibling spoke discouragingly to a young person. This should be avoided as much as possible as it has the tendency of resisting the growth of that seed within them.

Even when children make mistakes, they must be corrected in love. Punishments usually satisfies the punisher but may not yield any behavioral change. Parents and caretakers must take time to develop a healthy relationship with their children, set boundaries of control, explain to them their expectations, model good behavior and encourage them. That climate will yield more behavioral change than simply rebuking them.

> "There is a seed of greatness in every child that must be watered with kind and encouraging words."

In cases where children get out of control, seek help with counselling and remember the power of prayer to change things. Through prayer, rely on God the gift giver, to help protect your child and turn their hearts away from evil to good.

The story is told of a mother who had the boldness to reject the pronouncement of educators concerning his son as addled. Instead, she spoke kind and encouraging words to her son, and being a teacher herself homeschooled this little boy. This was the story of the great inventor, Thomas Edison.

Our world could possibly be without the phonograph, motion picture camera and the electric light bulb, some of the most powerful inventions of all time by Thomas Edison. His inventions revolutionized our industrialized world. If Thomas Edison did not have a mother who could intervene, and counter the negative words imposed on him by educators with love and kindness to nurture the greatness in him, the negative label could have destroyed the seed of greatness we saw in young Thomas.

Dear parent or guardian, will you stand in the place of Jesus and shape your child or the children under your care with kind and encouraging words? You have the power to make a difference.

Reflections

(After reading this chapter journal your thoughts or action plan)

Little Things, Big Results

"Little hinges swing big doors."

I first heard the quote above from one of my mentors, Dr. Mike Murdock. Little keys unlock huge gates, but very often we never recognize the impact that seemingly little things can have. Drops of water make a mighty ocean. A journey of a thousand miles begins with a step. **As little as little is, it must not be belittled, lightly treated, or ignored.** Small is the new big because small can always get you to big, and sometimes, the small things we ignore create or lead to the impact we expect to have with big things, especially when God is at work through that little thing.

Even God mostly speaks to us in a still *small* voice. Quietness is not necessarily a sign of a lack of power.

> "And he said, go forth, and stand upon the mount before the Lord. And, behold, the Lord passed by,

and a great and strong wind rent the mountains,
and brake in pieces the rocks before the Lord;
but the Lord was not in the wind: and after the
wind and earthquake; but the Lord was not in the
earthquake: And after the earthquake a fire; but
the Lord was not in the fire: and after the fire a
still small voice."

1 Kings 19:11–12 KJV

Anytime we brush off things of little measure as insignificant, we
stand the chance of missing out on reaping great results. If you
ignore little, you can never realize big. This subject is so critical
that God tests our faithfulness, not with the big stuff, but rather
in the little:

"If you are faithful in little things you will become
faithful in large ones."

Luke 16:10 NLT

Look at your life. What little thing have you belittled or failed to
recognize? It may be a little idea, a little suggestion, a little money,
or even a little child which seem unimportant to you. That little
thing or person you haven't given attention to may be your little
golden key to unlock the treasure house that leads to your destiny.
You may be dealing with a problematic issue which has been
stagnant for very long. It could be your health, your finances,
your relationship, meeting a deadline, launching that product, or
taking that leap into a new love relationship or business. But all
the while you're failing to make headway because you haven't paid
attention to a "little" suggestion or idea.

Such was the case of the army general of Syria, Naaman. As previously mentioned, he was a successful army general and a leader, but he was leprous. Although he was miraculously healed of his leprosy, this would not have been the case had he ignored the suggestion of a little maidservant. Who would have imagined that the key that unlocked the door to Naaman's healing was wrapped up in a little maid's suggestion? Most of us would have missed this.

I pray you aren't missing out on something great just because you have a preconceived, custom-fit style or method by which you expect solutions to come. Sometimes, that little suggestion, caution, or comment may be the "voice of God" in your given situation of need. Naaman's little maid's little suggestion led to a great and miraculous healing of leprosy.

Which little suggestion or voice around you are you failing to recognize?

We can also ignore little comments or contributions because they come from younger people or those of a lesser rank or status. Such deliberate or unconscious moves can sometimes delay or deny us our reward. Such a case is recorded in Acts 12, when the believers prayed earnestly for the deliverance of their bishop, Peter, who was in prison.

They were gathered at the house of Mary, the mother of the disciple John Mark. Although they were praying with expectation, they seemed not to have imagined receiving what seemed like an auto-response to their prayers. Seemingly instantly, Peter was released from jail miraculously by an angel of God.

At this point, the "little" feature has yet to show up, but once the answer to their prayers was at their door, little Rhoda was to be the first to get to the door. Although no loud doorbell rang, her propensity to jump at the sound of knocking is probably an indication of her "little" big faith anticipating the answer to their long hours of prayer. (If her going to the door was also a matter of duty expected of her as the youngest, then my hypothesis is flawed.) However, a lesson can still be learned from the reaction of the elders after little Rhoda returned from the door.

In that passage of scripture, the elderly folks did not seem expectant for such a miracle, or they fell for the "belittling trap" just because a young damsel was the one delivering the news. The severity of their actions would have been more graphic in this *Prison Break* episode if the captors had been pursuing the one who was fleeing. Their delay in believing Rhoda's report and hastening to get their bishop out of the cold as he stood outside would have cost the church of God austerely.

> "When we partner with Jesus, our small efforts become super exploits."

Don't ignore that little signal of good things yet to come. A glimmer of hope is in that little thing; recognize it. Little things can and do lead to big results, especially when God is at work through that little thing. It's a simple formula: when our small efforts encounter Jesus, they become super.

We see this happen in the feeding of the five thousand gathered on the mountain as recorded in John 6. The moment that a little boy in the crowd that afternoon was willing to release his little lunch meant that a meager five loaves of bread and two fish would become a mighty supply of food, enough to feed a massive crowd of over five thousand people with a dozen baskets full of bread left over! It was a jaw-dropping miracle produced from a meal that could be likened to a drop in the ocean considering the numbers to be fed.

But that is exactly what Jesus can do when you hand over your little to him.

Reflections

(After reading this chapter journal your thoughts or action plan)

God Can And
Will Use You!

Yes! God can and wants to use you.

The prerequisite for selection on God's super team will amaze you. If a team worth its salt needs to be created for any task, project, or competition, the selection criterion will be rigorous and, most likely, only the crème de la crème will make it on such a list. Think of a team to represent your school in a national quiz competition or a team to represent your country in the Olympic Games, etc. The screening process will be a case of the survival of the fittest, smartest, fastest, and most knowledgeable, as the case might be. Indeed, only the best of the best will appear on the final list and there will be no place for the amateur, the weak, and the unlearned. So, if imperfect man has these standards of meritocracy, perhaps God's standard may even be higher and there's no chance for anything but the best and super brilliant. But that is not exactly the case so don't lose hope.

See, with God, it is not as if He does not desire excellence and competence. Far from that; He desires to show forth His Glory in and through us.

> "But we have this treasure in earthen vessels that the excellence of the power may be of God and not of us."

> 2 Corinthians 4:7

God has the prerogative to use anyone or anything as He desires to accomplish His purposes. For that task ahead, that project or competition, and for the grand purpose of your entire life, God's desire is to show forth His Glory, and He will use anyone He desires who is available, irrespective of the standard placed on them by other men or themselves, for His glorious purposes.

> "But God has chosen the foolish things of the world to put to shame the wise, and God has chosen the weak things of the world to put to shame the things which are mighty."

> 1 Corinthians 1:27

So why does God choose foolish and weak things? So that no one can boast in His presence (1 Corinthians 1:29). It's never about us; everything in this life is about God and we were made for His glory. The weak become strong in the hands of God, and that confounds the mighty. When God chooses to use you, the mighty will be put to shame by the transformation that has occurred in your life.

From the last passage we read, 1 Corinthians 1:27, we see five categories of people or things which the world would normally reject and classify as unqualified for God's use:

- the foolish
- the weak
- the base/low things
- the despised
- and things which are not.

But God explicitly states these same classes of people are fit for His use.

Have you ever been tagged as foolish, not-so-smart, stupid, or dumb by others? Do others describe you as weak or unable to accomplish any task? Would you describe yourself that way? Have you been relegated to the base of the ladder or the bottom of the pyramid? Have you been classified as low? Are you despised and abused and not considered an entity within your community?

Don't bow your head in shame or accept this naming as true. God uses people just like you and me to do the great and mighty things which baffle the so-called experts who are believed to be the wise and strong people of this world.

Do you know that when the world calls you all those names, they are just trying to force you into becoming or behaving like someone you are not? You are unique; you cannot live your life trying to be like someone else. If you reject the wrong naming and labeling and embrace your uniqueness as defined in the person of Jesus Christ, you will find your true worth and significance.

Wherever you are or whatever you find yourself doing, you can now begin to do it with purpose and strive to excel in that.

You will become such a fierce person whom no one can match up to when you begin to live the special purpose God created you for. This gives Him pleasure. Don't allow the world to force you into its mold. You are not a cosmic accident; you are His masterpiece.

> "For we are God's masterpiece. He has created us anew in Christ Jesus, so we can do the good things he planned for us long ago."
>
> Ephesians 2:10 NLT

If God used Rahab, the prostitute, He can and will use you. If God used Moses, a murderer and stammerer, He can and will use you. If God used the shepherd boy David, despite being despised by his own family, and raised him up to become the king of Israel and the earthly grandfather of Jesus, He can and will use you.

If He even used animals and things, like Balaam's donkey (Numbers 22:21–39), a jawbone in the hands of Samson (Judges 15:14–17), and five loaves of bread and two fish in the hands of Jesus (Matthew 14:13–21), my dear friend, God can and will use you!

You Are Not an Accident

The circumstances surrounding the birth of some people or the events happening around them may cause them to scoff at the chance of God using them for anything significant, but this is what I want you to know: you are not an accident, and God has specially planned you for His glory. He can use everything about you to bring forth praise to His name. This is what God says about you in His Word:

> "I am your creator. You were in my care even before you were born."
>
> Isaiah 44:2 CEV

Believe the Word of God and live up to it. Let the character of your heart be one that is true, genuine, and sincere. God looks at the heart and will use you. Even if you are not the most eloquent or skilled per the world's standards, God is the master architect of your life, and He is working out His plan with your life.

> "You, (God), saw me before I was born and scheduled each day of my life before I began to breathe. Every day was recorded in your book!"
>
> Psalm 139:16 TLB, emphasis mine

Be Humble

It may surprise you, but in as much as God desires to use you and me, He rejects some people. These are people who solely trust in their own ability, knowledge, experience, skill, etc. to achieve what they believe is the purpose of their lives. The Bible calls them "the proud." (Proverbs 3:34, 1 Peter 5:5b)). They believe it is all about them, and they do not accord God the recognition as the Giver of life and Sustainer of all things. To them, everything starts and ends with them. They may even scoff at or ridicule the idea of the Almighty God as our creator and absolute authority of life. Their eyes have been blinded to the truth of God's Word and His plan of salvation. They are proud and God will not use them.

> "But He gives more grace. Therefore He says: 'God resists the proud, But gives grace to the humble.'"

> James 4:6

Uzziah was merely a teenager when he became the king of Judah after the death of his father Amaziah (2 Chronicles 26). This young man pleased God and did exploits during his reign, but he could not stay humble. Pride led to his destruction. King Uzziah overstepped his bounds, broke protocol by entering into the holy place of Gods' temple and performing the duty of a priest.

> His fame spread far and wide, for the Lord gave him marvelous help, and he became very powerful. But when he had become powerful, he also became proud, which led to his downfall. He sinned against the Lord his God by entering the sanctuary of the Lord's Temple and personally burning incense on the incense altar. Azariah the high priest went in after him with eighty other priests of the Lord, all brave men. They confronted King Uzziah and said, "It is not for you, Uzziah, to burn incense to the Lord. That is the work of the priests alone, the descendants of Aaron who are set apart for this work. Get out of the sanctuary, for you have sinned. The Lord God will not honor you for this!" Uzziah, who was holding an incense burner, became furious. But as he was standing there raging at the priests before the incense altar

in the Lord's Temple, leprosy suddenly broke out on his forehead. When Azariah the high priest and all the other priests saw the leprosy, they rushed him out. And the king himself was eager to get out because the Lord had struck him. So King Uzziah had leprosy until the day he died. He lived in isolation in a separate house, for he was excluded from the Temple of the Lord. His son Jotham was put in charge of the royal palace, and he governed the people of the land. The rest of the events of Uzziah's reign, from beginning to end, are recorded by the prophet Isaiah son of Amoz. When Uzziah died, he was buried with his ancestors; his grave was in a nearby burial field belonging to the kings, for the people said, "He had leprosy." And his son Jotham became the next king.

2 Chronicles 26:15b – 23 NLT

> "Be humble to remain in your place
> of influence and secured to allow
> others function in theirs."

My dear brother/sister, always remember to ascribe all glory to God, be humble to stay in your place and secured to allow others to function in theirs. Avoid the mistake of Uzziah and others who erred in like manner.

Be Willing

This requirement is critical because if God didn't want your cooperation, He would have just created robots and had them do whatever He desired. But because He wants us to say yes to His will without compulsion, He created us free moral agents who have the liberty to choose their actions and bear full responsibility for any repercussions.

Our willingness then proves that our obedience to do God's will is from an open heart. One can also obey a command without wholeheartedly wanting to do so. With God, what really matters is not that you did His will alone, but that you did His will with a free and cheerful heart.

Opening our hearts and stretching our hands to meet God's is our way of saying, "I will, Lord. Use me." Once you do this, you are an eligible candidate for the master's use.

> "If ye be **willing and obedient** you shall eat the good of the land."
>
> Isaiah 1:19, emphasis added

Be Obedient

Obedience is key to God using us. Willingness and obedience must go hand in hand. You can be willing but end up not obeying. Obedience then is the visible feature of an inward state of being or decision. **When your heart is willing, your hands must work it out to prove that you truly obey.** The Apostle James's description of faith without works is a classic way to explain obedience to a person who says he is willing yet does not obey (James 2:14 – 26).

As I discussed in the "Grace for Guilt" section of an earlier chapter, we are sometimes held back by fear, and this can cause us not to take that step of obedience. No matter what causes fear, it will let you count yourself out of God's plan for your life. Fear makes us feel unworthy, unloved, unqualified, unaccepted, and unforgiven. I love this mnemonic of fear:

False

Evidence

Appearing

Real

The fear isn't real. Face it head-on with the Word of Faith and you will win.

Ananias, who was unheard of before Acts 9, was very fearful (and rightly so) when God instructed him through a vision to go and pray for Saul's healing. Ananias was afraid because of what he had heard concerning Saul, but notice that he still obeyed. Saul was a dreadful killer and fierce rival of the faith who fought against the believers of his time. Although Ananias resisted and struggled, he managed to confront his fears and went to pray for Saul as God directed. Consequently, a great miracle of healing and salvation occurred for Saul.

Ananias went further by introducing Saul to the body of believers and this introduction was the beginning of a great ministry.

Although some theologians believe Ananias should have mentored Saul a bit more regarding his obedience to the voice of God amidst the fears he had, we see a good example of how that step of faith dissipates fear. Face your fears, step out in faith, and see God move!

Peter also faced his fears. Thinking they had seen a ghost, the eleven other disciples were stuck in a boat because of fear. Nevertheless, upon Jesus's command, Peter stepped out in faith and actually walked on water! (Matthew 14:22–33).

Even Jesus had to overcome his fears and embrace his assignment. Toward the climax of his earthly ministry, He was scared to death and wished somehow to escape the cup of suffering. But He did not bow to fear. Rather, He moved on to obey the calling on His life and drank the cup of suffering by embracing death on the cross.

Be Available

You are where you are for a purpose. Rahab's location in Jericho was strategic (probably for the profession she was engaged in), yet that place was also strategic for connecting her with God's people and ultimately saving her life as well.

The maid in Naaman's house was in a good spot for God to use as a channel of blessing to her master. Once you understand this fact, your mission is to be available wherever you find yourself, knowing it is a place from which God can and wants to use you.

Right in that home, that neighborhood, that office, or that class, God wants to use you. Be available. To some extent, your gifts, talents, and uniqueness do not matter much if you are not available. You can be a blessing to the world or a solution to a problem if you are where you're needed most. "If only I were there, I could have solved that problem" shouldn't be the case you find yourself in. When you have been gifted by God and placed in a place for His purpose, yet you seem to be distracted and never in a position to do what you can do, God will use an available person, irrespective of how better you think you are compared to them.

Many people have had their golden chance of being part of something big which they weren't initially meant to be a part of, but because someone wasn't available, they got the chance to try out a role or activity and ended up doing it, sometimes even better on a first attempt or over time than the original cast the role was intended for. Sometimes, all you must do is just be around. You may be required to run errands, do menial tasks, keep the door, etc. Whatever it is, just be around. You may be the next in line for a miracle.

Availability is such a priceless gift. That is why God said His Spirit will always be with us. Be available.

His Timings and Guidance

> "It is not in man who walks to direct his own steps."
>
> Jeremiah 10:23b

> "The steps of a good man are ordered by the Lord, and He delights in his way."
>
> Psalm 37:23

Although careful planning is essential, it will not always guarantee success unless you totally commit your ways to God and trust Him to put you in the right place at the right time for His perfect will to be accomplished in your life. The phrase "right place at the right time" is rendered in Hebrew as *qarah*.

If being available is so important, you don't just want to be available; you want to be available at the place where you are most needed and your gifts and talents most appreciated. You want to be at the right place at the right time (*qarah*), and that can only happen when God truly orders your steps—not by mere happenstance, but by God's guidance. This is similar to how a misfortune may happen to someone by virtue of their location at the scene of an accident, in which case we may say they found themselves at the wrong place at the wrong time. However we may not logically comprehend how all events occur. In a better sense, God ordains good things to happen to you by leading you to be at the right place at the right time.

Make it a prayer and believe God for *qarah*. It is divine order, alignment, and precision. The hand of God puts you where you ought to be and not where you want to be. God can use you. All you need is *qarah*.

A Time for Everything

> "For everything there is a season, and a time for every purpose under heaven."

> Ecclesiastes 3:1

I want you to remember this: You do not live forever on earth! We are here temporarily and on a specific, time-bound assignment.

When it comes to God using us, we must not be the ones to dictate the appropriate time for God to use us. Sometimes, we know in our hearts what God is calling us to do. It could be a ministry of teaching and preaching, caring for preschoolers, sharing our experiences and knowledge as a counselor, or starting a nonprofit or a profit-making business venture. Whatever it is you believe God is calling you to do, do not push it aside with the "I'm not ready" excuse and give God a certain time you feel you will be ready.

Some have a call to full-time pulpit ministry, but they believe they will be better suited for it after they have amassed a certain amount of money from a secular job. They tell God, "Just wait till I'm forty, and I will really serve you," or, "After I marry, I will really serve God." Others give excuses for many things God wants to use them for. Some feel they first need to be a certain age, have a certain pedigree, be at a certain place, or own certain things. In deciding the timing for when God can use us, let us always give God the priority in helping us make this critical life-changing decision.

There is a season for every purpose and timing for each season. So that we do not miss our timings for what God wants to do with our lives, we must be sensitive to the leadership and promptings of God's Spirit. When the season is right and God is calling you to embrace a specific assignment, you can always bank on the peace of God, which you will feel in your heart as surety of God's presence and guidance in that matter.

"And let the peace of God rule in your hearts, to which also you were called in one body; and be thankful."

Colossians 3:15

When we sense God's peace, even if all the details remain yet unknown, we can take that step of faith. This assurance of God's peace is a way He guides and leads us by His Spirit, and we must be grateful for this gift.

Be Thankful

"So then it is not of him who wills, nor of him who runs, but of God who shows mercy."

Romans 9:16

We must count it a privilege when God uses us, and we must be thankful.

The Bible entreats us to be thankful in all situations for that is God's will for us and it pleases Him (1 Thessalonians 5:18).

We can attract God's favor and selection by remaining thankful. Thanksgiving unlocks the heavens and makes God receptive to us. It is also a statement of faith when we thank God even before we say anything else to Him. Jesus always practiced this when He was on earth. He thanked God when He was faced with the Herculean task of raising dead Lazarus back to life (John 11:1–44). Before making a request of His Father, Jesus thanked Him. Again, when Jesus was about to feed five thousand men with five loaves and two fish, He thanked God first (John 6:1–14). We can learn from these examples that thanksgiving is an expression of faith and confidence in the power of God to perform even before we make a request.

God expects thanksgiving. It is courteous, and He is a gentleman and a God of order, so He expects us to deal with Him as such. Much more, thanksgiving completes or perfects our miracle. When the ten lepers were cleansed in Luke 17:11–19, only one of them came back to say thank you, and Jesus was very pleased with him. Why was Jesus so pleased with this? Because He expected them to show appreciation and gratitude. But we also see that the blessings we receive may not be perfected until we have shown appreciation for it. After the leper had come to thank Jesus, Jesus blessed him indeed, and by His words Jesus completely perfected the miracle and blessing of healing which the leper had already received. When we say a heartfelt 'thank you' for every opportunity to be used by God, to serve others, or even to receive help, we complete, perfect, and establish the miracle and blessing of God which comes upon us.

God is the Big Boss

> "Therefore God has mercy on whom he wants to have mercy, and he hardens whom he wants to harden."
>
> Romans 9:18 NIV

> "The Lord has made everything for his own purposes, even the wicked for a day of disaster."
>
> Proverbs 16:4 NLT

God is the potter; we are the clay. He is in control and all power belongs to Him. God has a bigger plan, and He calls men and women to partake in that grand program. We become coworkers with Him in accomplishing such a feat. When we submit our will to God's purpose and become involved in His plan, it is a great honor for us. We must always be grateful—grateful to be alive and to have the opportunity to be involved in God's agenda for our world today through our various vocations. We must embrace this opportunity as our calling and be grateful for it.

FINALLY

God is not necessarily looking for the sophisticated, but the simple, not the expert, but the teachable and willing learner, not the saint, but one who is sincere, even if he be a sinner. Be humble, avail yourself, and you will make it on God's team.

God can and will use you!

My Prayer for You

Thank you, Lord, for my life. Thank you for creating me in your image and likeness. I am complete in You, and all that concerns me is perfected. Thank you for your love, mercy, and grace. I rely not on my own strength, but I trust you to use me in any situation I find myself to be a problem solver. May I be an answer to someone's need, a blessing and not a burden, and show forth your praise through me.

"Take my life and let it be / Consecrated, Lord, to Thee. / Take my moments and my days, / Let them flow in endless praise."

Reflections

(After reading this chapter journal your thoughts or action plan)

Notes

Endnotes

1. Warren, Rick. Facebook post. April 20, 2016. https://www.facebook.com/pastorrickwarren/posts/10154038110710903:0

2. Colin Brown, ed., *The New International Dictionary of NT Theology, Vol. 1* (Grand Rapids: Zondervan, 1985).

Printed in the United States
by Baker & Taylor Publisher Services